Horse-Man

Em Strang

Horse-Man

Shearsman Books

First published in the United Kingdom in 2019 by
Shearsman Books
50 Westons Hill Drive
Emersons Green
BRISTOL
BS16 7DF

Shearsman Books Ltd Registered Office
30–31 St. James Place, Mangotsfield, Bristol BS16 9JB
(this address not for correspondence)

www.shearsman.com

ISBN 978-1-84861-677-6

Contents

For Horse-Man

The heart that loves me is a wound without shield
— Jalal-ud-Din Rumi

Yet earth contains
The horse as a remembrancer of wild
Arenas we avoid

— James Wright

Memory of a Boat Before I Was Born

I pray all day alone in the high mountains, sitting or lying down in a dark cave, where goats sometimes sleep and give birth. At the mouth of the cave, tall grasses grow and a sweet, wild lettuce that goats love. I am not the oldest animal in the cave, but it takes the sun a long time to filter in.

As night comes, I climb down into the valley, to the dark shore where the boat bobs. This is an old lake with bright fish that sing, and its water is wide and open. Old friends have met here, and lovers. This is a place for all kinds of lovers.

I stand still for some time, perhaps many years – while the lake empties and refills – and then I step carefully into the boat, let myself be carried out across the water to the place of my birth.

I.M. Big John Chang

I knew Big John Chang from the time he was young and fit, and full like a well-loved dog.

He had a face that shone out – lit up our faces, us brothers, even though we weren't his real brothers and I was a girl.

He wore the same blue fleece jacket for two years solid and a pair of trousers that were older than him.

I knew him before the drowning: sun for a face on weekdays, moon for a face at weekends, the kind of sun and moon you could rely on for brilliance. I've said that already.

If I knew him now, I'd say, 'All your light won't fit the boat; it'll spill out from your clothes, your eyes, your skin, and the whole lake will blaze and pulse from you like ripples from a rock.'

Maybe I'd say that.

The Lamp

The lamp is hot and white and almost sings
as you scrape a tiny hollow in the snow.
The light streams out towards you from all things.

You're bigger than you thought with arms like wings
that quiver in the space and seem to grow.
The lamp is hot and white and almost sings.

This lamp is like a drunken eye that swings,
pointing out the night you think you know.
The light streams out towards you from all things.

It's when the fox comes out that night begins
as in your heart a red wind starts to blow.
The lamp is hot and white and almost sings.

You cannot know the morning, what it brings
until the fox has melted with the snow.
The light streams out towards you from all things.

You gather up the night beneath your wings
and let it stab your self from head to toe.
The lamp is hot and white and almost sings.

When the night has passed, the cold air stings
and somewhere in a pine tree sits a crow.
The light streams out towards you from all things.

You didn't ask for this, such tender skin
with a newness that was born so long ago.
The lamp is hot and white and almost sings.
The light streams out towards you from all things.

Dark River, Dusk

White bull on the riverbank
leaning its bulk weight
on a steep, perpendicular line
to the water.

It slips slowly in
or the river sips and laps the bull.
Its white rump burns out.

Two Cows

Where the sun comes in across the grass
like a snake comes, silently, smoothly
because this is its habit –
two white cows.

The cows stand
with their hooves on the earth
like the feet of great tables.

Their backs bear the weight
of unbroken sunlight
from beginning to end.

Their bodies carry the myth of light
long after dusk.

They stand and stand.

Most Beautiful Bull

Disciples must make up their mind to overpower the bull; that is, they must learn to control the untamed, brutal, violent force of their sensuality so as to make use of its strength. To overpower the bull does not mean to kill it; if you kill it you will not be able to benefit from its strength.
—Omraam Mikhaël Aïvanhov

Most beautiful bull,
you stake out your place.

When I listen to you
I hear patience, deeper

than the field's furrow,
but not by much.

You roar here at the hedge,
brown bulk, small pig eyes.

Most beautiful bull,
you wield your girder.

Talking Meat

I'm quite still. I turn to look
but it's too dark to tell the time
and I'm smaller than usual.
I have, in fact, no body at all.
At the bottom of the bed, joints of meat
laid out from right to left
like stillborn infants in an ante-chamber.
Massive legs of lamb or pork or beef
with the skin still on and bristles
to remind us of animals.
'It's OK. Don't be afraid!' they say.
But I am afraid and there's a rattle
at the back of my throat, a low growl
like a starving dog with a femur.
Even without eyes, I have a clear view
of each cut. Even without a nose,
I can smell the fresh high scent of death
as though it were my own. Each limb
is dripping, tepid in the breath of the room.
I reach for something – water, daylight –
but there is no reaching, only someone else's fingers
like a rack of ribs off a palm.

At the Delicatessen with Gaping Wound

I want this meat and these loaves.
Big leg of lamb and red rack of pork.

The fat around the muscle is odious,
white like a smoker's sclera.

I see the fresh bread is brooding
and there's a row of knives like dead fish.

The man lifts everything
deftly over the counter.

There has never been meat in my life
nor loaves like these.

The man sees that the pork will fit the gash
and the bread will swab the blood.

I look up as I shove the things in.
How much?

Slaughterhouse

Those white hands working a dark space
of universal muscle over universal bone.

Somewhere a barn door opens and closes.

Dogs with bright faces bark for so long
that the dust turns back into stone.

This Dog Barking

This dog barking from ten fields off
in the single bud of night,
is the time you forgot your mother.

It's easy and hard
like the wind off the hill blowing through
like wind blows, ready
to swallow sound for the throat's sake.

This dog knows the way
sound carries years over grass,
each nighttime bark a beacon
from some white stone farmhouse with barns.

You listen with late night ears
and a small white face, bare arms.

Perhaps you're not really this daughter.

This dog barking from ten fields off
is the empty chair in the delicate house
where nobody waits for your call.

Nobody's waiting to taste the cool water
from the white cup you loved as a child.

Elegy

I'm sick of living nicely with this pain,
as though my face is honest facing you.
The thunder drums like horses, but no rain.

I light a candle quietly in your name
and listen as you settle in a pew.
I'm sick of living nicely with this pain.

If I was good, I'd hang my head in shame
and bite my tongue so hard it split in two.
But I'm sick of living nicely with this pain.

I'll dig a shallow grave to bury blame –
my friends will show me what I have to do.
The thunder drums like horses, but no rain.

And afterwards we'll cry and sing the same,
I'll wait for you to tell me love is true.
I'm sick of living nicely with this pain.

We can put a pretty picture in a frame
but it isn't how it is with me and you.
I'm sick of living nicely with this pain.
The thunder drums like horses, but no rain.

Bus-dog's Lesson on Grief

I'm on number 33 and it's sunny.
The light is coming in and the heat,
so much light and heat, I'd prefer
to shut my eyes and sleep,
not get off at the cemetery to lay flowers,
not kneel at her graveside and sob;
I'd prefer almost anything to that.

It's because I look down – Jesus God! –
I look down and see my legs
have become dog legs,
my feet have become dog feet,
those tough, rusky pads
scuffing the floor of the bus,
those unclipped claws
like good new moons.

'Nice legs,' the girl beside me says, 'May I?'
I nod and she leans down to stroke.
These are fine, coarse brown fur legs,
short-haired but the coat is thick,
the fur is strong and smells musky, doggy.
'Lovely,' she says, 'lovely, strong legs.'

It's because her hands are warm and soft,
her hands are heavy feathers,
that I sit quite still,
let her stroke my new dog legs.
'The next stop's mine,' I say,
wishing she would stroke forever.

I feel the urge to stretch out my legs,
to lie down in the aisle between seats
with my arms above my head
and my legs and feet
out long in front.

It's because I want my belly to be free.
I want all of me to be free
for stroking.

'This is it,' she says, 'the next stop.'
I get up from my seat,
thank her somewhat gruffly
and walk to the front of number 33.
My new legs walk me.
My new feet trot.

Something changes as I jump off,
a kind of distension and drop –
I see my arms too are rearranged,
that now I have no arms
and in their place are dog legs.

It's because my sister is waving at the gate
that I walk over on all fours.
The feeling is pleasant.
My face is nearer the ground
than it's ever been before.

'Hello,' she says, and we run together
up and down the long rows of graves.

The Art of Emptiness

For Kath

You never know, you might fall into a room
so big even a pack of dogs would lose themselves
in its over-familiar corners, its bright lights
and smooth white walls. Even the floor
might fool you into thinking it led somewhere
you'd never been before, somewhere new
and untrodden, first snow, arctic blue
so bright it hurts your eyes. But no,
the room is only what you thought was there.
You stretch out your arms and meet the air
in all directions, and as you turn your body
to and fro, the dogs gather like budburst,
carry you out on their sweet, strong backs,
and as you ride into the streets and out
into the woods and hills, you know for sure
there's no such thing as rooms
nor the things we put in them day after day.
And so the dogs melt and the ground falls away.

Capreolus Capreolus

They make their way into the heart of the roughest solitudes
                    – John Muir

Not quite knowing how,
I close the door to the house,

push out into air as though I'm bursting
the membrane of an egg.

It's cold and the ground taps back my steps,
makes brief sense of this leaving.

It's true, I have a small blue coat
and a hat made of stone.

In every tree a woodpigeon coos
as though we all love one another.

I walk with your face in my pocket.
The trees bend and blow about.

There are no friendly roe deer
with forked antlers and coarse hair.

Inside the house,
they're laying your body out.

Passage

This evening, the cold East wind
and a dozen deer – ten hinds –

on the shore at low tide.
They time everything

by the line of the sea on the rocks
and the sea's temperature,

immersing themselves
like small brown suns.

Nobody sees them cross
from mainland to island, moving

as though they're the first boats
to be dreamt,

and nobody needs to see them
to know

this crossing is one mile long
or perhaps twenty.

The sun is almost down
beneath the sea.

One stag leads
and the other follows,

or the hinds swim ahead –
it doesn't matter.

There's time to breathe
and move like good swimmers

towards a shore which is neither
here nor there, especially when it rains.

Nobody sees them land, bodies sodden
with the weight of saltwater,

and they shake like dogs
in the slack eye of night.

Old Photograph

Here are my parents:
one in a tailor-made black suit,
the other only half visible through fog –
that slow institute of grief.
I turn the photo over, let them go
their inexorable ways,
like the Dodo and the Black Spider Monkey –
my mother an endangered species,
my father long extinct.

But inside my mind's eye, I call the Dodo.
I call the Black Spider Monkey from deep down
in the hunger of things.

Voice

Only bring the hunger that you are, the hidden
star in your throat,
that dark beacon.

Bog Iris

The peace the world cannot give (John 14:27)

These quiet and silent flowers
have everything to say about love,
even when I'm hunched in the grass
pretending to be them; particularly then.

Daily Bread

The danger is not that the soul should doubt whether there is any bread,
but that, by a lie, it should persuade itself it is not hungry —Simone Weil

Marya:

To begin with, the breath

[...]

To begin with the breath
and the wind blowing, rain coming in
like good news, grass growing.

[...]

But all too soon, a high-pitched, wizened sound
not from the mouth, but the body.
Dark brown mostly, with eight stripy legs
all quaking in the heat.
Exsiccated, dehydrated, fried.
Even spiders need water to survive.

I'd been dreaming every night of the animals,
most of them either scared or dying,
white with suffering.
I don't know but I can see it in their flesh,
in the way they move their limbs by day,
in the way their breath ticks by night.
It's how it is with so many.
The longing that sits on the outside of the skin,
so visible, if you allow it.

When the heat came the skin sizzled,
formed blisters like jellyfish.

The heat restrained us
but made us stronger.
It's a strange thing to learn –
that sudden lack takes you back
to being human,
nothing to hold on to,
no control, no overview.
You have to let it burn your roots!

It's like being inside a flame
all day and all night,
as though each time you breathe
you're intensifying, feeding on fire,
tongue of magma.
The same white heat melts the lungs
as they speak in crackling waves of lack,
as though their whole lives
have been about a missing piece,
a search for a single, essential alveolus
that knows a different way of breathing.

When your skin begins to blister and flake,
the memory of cold water breaks out.
Your lungs whimper softly and each organ,
including the skin, begins to shout in furious tongues
as though they're finally done with being ignored.
Imagine it! What does the heart say?

[...]

Father's heart is a strange beast.
I can see through it,
as though I've eyes in each ventricle.
It's like I'm the bloody muscle
that pumps his life in.
It's sick really, parasitic.
Or it's just what it is;
it's the way the lake's a lake one minute
and the next, a crater;
the way the heart's an empty box,
waiting for something to fill it.

Toxic stories, I've seen them
hitch like fish hooks in the heart,
in the cavity where God used to be,
the part we never needed to name.
Stories that make you think you're whole
when you're not.

One night I dreamt the wheat fields were alight.
There were black cows, hundreds of them,
crammed in so tight the wire fence cut their flanks.
The entire crop had been trampled flat.
They squirmed there, bleating,
fire melting the skin off their backs.
And in the next field, people
stretched out in the heat, relaxed.

Touch dead flesh by day or in a dream,
and you can tell how the animal lived,
what it loved, how deep its pain ran.
It comes in feelings and pictograms.

It isn't easy or clear-cut,
but when you stop being thick-skinned,
when you finally co-opt the pain,
you know why you're here,
and it's not what you think.

[...]

Father:

She's gone to grass,
the last blades in this burnt-out place,
where everything finally cedes
to the dust, except her.
If the past has a voice,
it belongs, no doubt, to Marya.

She's deep down like a former life,
somewhere sleepy, ancient.
But her mouth's still there,
pursed maybe, silky with spiders
or worse.

Some days I still stand and speak,
tell her how nice her hair,
tell her she's tender, sweet.

I remember the women,
talking bread and hair in the heat.

We know heat here.
Gets so hot your blood shouts –
Too little! Too late! –

and a neighbour watches as your skin melts,
as the timber of your house curls up
like stale crusts for the birds.
Vultures.

Inside's better than out,
since there's no shade
and no breeze to breathe with.
But you can't lie down all day
doing nothing –
there's food to be found
or a tub of water for a wash.

Slim pickings, and no way to plough
a different furrow.

Too late for that,
and now this.

The ground's cracked, inch wide gaps
that lead down deep
to nothing.

No subsoil, just rock and the far off silence
of once-upon-a-time water.
It makes you itch.
It's as though the earth is your skin,
its rifts and ridges your cracking epidermis,
as though you've a bad case of eczema
or erysipelas, skin canyons,
a whole geography of pain and lack.

Three years I've been coming back
and the memories don't fade, the pictures.
The mind's eye holds things just fine.
Sometimes.

[...]

You can walk up to the ditch where the river was,
the widest part can fit at least five men head to heel
and it used to flow at least one and a half men deep.
Picture that! A whole beast of water
with the mountain in its throat
and the sea in its gut, roaring out
as though God had gruffly ordered it,
like a father to his adolescent daughter.
Oh boy, that was some river!

This is my land, my farm.
It's not much. It's rusty.
It smells of hot planks
and burnt dust.
It's rickety.

There are four graves now
and I would tell you how they came
and who they house. But I can't.

I'll tell what went before,
if my throat lasts without water.
I'll tell you this one: my youngest daughter

[...]

She never took no for an answer,
never lied, strode like a horse strides,
gracious, bold, with her head high,
even when the drought came
and the baby died.
Even then.

Marya crowned me.
She made me come alive, lit me up,
helped me step into this new skin
in spite of the increasing heat and dust,
in spite of the lack. She was my waterfall,
and I stood beneath her and drank.

In early spring we had black-eyed beans in the backfield,
where the water used to run and the mustard grew.
A small patch in full sun, manageable,
with a long view to the south.
The women worked it mostly,
Marya amongst them, tallest, leanest,
mouth like a ruby, polished.

I used to watch them pick,
small hands like songbirds
in and out the canes,
plucking beans into buckets,
rearranging their hands as the sweat ran.

I used to listen to them sweating,
until the day Marya told me
they always listened to me listening.

She had brown skin and black hair
and that's how I loved her.
Just as she was.
No additives, I used to say.
No preservatives.

[...]

My small farm grew wheat,
twenty-five seeds per square foot.
Golden grains, stems three feet high.
In the days before drought
we'd make enough to survive,
truck the crop away,
buy bread.

Nobody said it wouldn't last.

We had to thresh and winnow it
by hand in the end.
It was a full-time job for one man
to feed his family daily bread.
We ground it with old stone, rocks
like molars with the bite smoothed off.
It made me want my past over again, that wheat;
it made living weary, tight.

She was born three years before
the drought kicked in.
Sickly at first, more gurny gob
than any baby I'd known.
She'd wake every ten minutes bawling,

mouth wide like a limpet stuck on a rock,
a dark, rubbery persistence.

Chip off the old block,
that's what Nura said.
We had to take her in shifts, she and I,
and one night, so sleep-deprived,
so open with exhaustion,
something happened –
an aberration, a distortion.

The light was weird.
The fields looked edged with light, glowing,
as though heaven was in them or God
or something out there combusting, igniting.
My wheat glowed,
as though it was radioactive, luminous.

Is this it, I thought, doom finally come?
But no.
There was a sense of infinite grief
together with wellbeing, even peace.

After that, we surrendered to it, Nura and I;
we stuck at it for a long time,
in sickness and in health.
We forgave each other our trespasses
as best we could,
Nura huddled over her crucifix.
She said the wood understood
better than the flesh.

[...]

Three years I've been coming back,
and the one truth I've learnt,
is that we keep speaking, all of us,
whether we're living or not.

If we use the voice to bury the dying,
can we use it to sing them back?

She died on a Tuesday.
The memory's like an object,
a rough stone in a tight fist.
The baby had been dead some time,
maybe a year, maybe more.

It was an angry death:
nothing I did to soothe her was enough.

Tuesday and the heat was so severe
I thought my chest might cave in.
Marya had been unwell for weeks,
dehydrated, limbs spider-thin.
She lay there sighing, crying small names –
the baby's, her mother's.

There was nothing I could do to make it stop.

Tuesday and I tidied the last items
we owned – bed, bowl, bible – and left her
in search of water.

Tuesday and I walked out barefoot.
I remember because the ground was hot.
The sun was up and up and up.

I walked a long time,
out towards the last scrap of trees
where there used to be water and no hunger;
to the old well we dug when the rains stopped
and the river dried.

Tuesday and I looked for hours,
half the day, maybe more,
and when I returned to her
with nothing
and my own breath barely drawing,
I knew she was gone;
that I'd failed her completely;
that she'd never forgive me.

And it stuck in my throat like a feather,
white in the red of my mouth,
one that has grown there silently
that I can't quite swallow.

Shall I open wide and show you?

[...]

She lay like an empty sack
with her mouth open
and her teeth showing,
as though she wanted to get back
at the world one last time,
or at me.
Some father.

Marya:

[…]

It's late and I'm almost done.
There's a cart waiting outside,
hand-made with rough planks,
thick with sunlight and dust.

If I look closely, which I do,
I can see my name baked into the wood.

I'm half asleep, half awake,
and the figure in the room
is not Father.

The air is hot
as it always is, and the roof
is lifting up and back, up and back
as though it's a pair of black wings
and I'm lying in the body of a bird.

The figure moves around the bed
its head bent, hovering in one corner
and then the other.

It exits, then comes back in
pushing the cart ahead.

When I look down at my body on the bed,
I see clouds – not worms, not blood,
not a grisly rack of bones,

but clouds so full of light
I have to squint.

Where my legs were,
are now immaculate clouds.
Where my torso was, clouds.
Where my arms were, clouds.
They move gently, rising and falling.

I want to share this new cloud truth,
to hold the hand of Father or the hand of Nura,
or the hands of my brothers and sisters.
In my cloud-arms I could hold my baby.

But there's just me
and the figure with the cart by the bed.
There's just enough time for the figure
to bend forward and lift my cloud-head.

[...]

We're outside now and travelling fast.
The air is muggy, dense, and each time the wheels turn,
one of my cloud-parts begins its ascent.

The figure pushes the cart to a low shack like ours,
and as we draw near I can see the open door,
hear the shift of dust on the wooden boards.

We park as though we've an appointment.

Inside, the space is dark
but I can hear something rustling,

some nearby, hidden thing
that knows about forgiving.

Then I see the white feather I saved,
the one with the good, strong quill
that always fanned a breeze,
no matter how still the day.

By the time I see his tired face,
our whole lives have passed.
Father lifts up the feather
and wafts it gently to and fro.
I'm going now, I say.
Yes, he says, *I know*.

[...]

Peony

Fearless,
the peony has fully opened and is
the deepest vermilion pompom.
It hangs in the long grass
like a bloody fist or a fresh heart.

Leveret

We have been busy accumulating solace. Make us afraid of how we were.
—Jalal-ud-Din Rumi

I lift you up, though you're mostly dead.
I'm scared to finish you, in case I'm good at it.
I talk as though you're a baby dying.
I keep talking anyway.

The verge is green from summer rain.
I put you in the foot-well, the cave of your crossing.
Your body is a fur boot, hand-stitched, native.
Still, I drive you ten fields off.

In the front yard, you are beheaded.
Your legs twitch once or twice.

I can't believe it has come to this.
If I had the courage, I'd nurse you back to health.

Loneliness

I don't worry about it anymore.
I can go out
to feed the hens and collect eggs
and not worry if it's enough.
A scattering of corn
and they gather the rest –
small bugs, worms, grass.
It's not my serving that matters.
I stand in the mud and so do they.

At Stoker's Cottage

For Frank

I wake to the way the sea comes in
to the land and the birds wait
on the edge of first light.

I go outside to chop wood.

The earth is so attentive
it shocks me along the path
to the axe and the block.

My hand is the beginning
and ending of every woman's hand,
and my heart is the round of wood
as I lay it down, knowing
almost nothing.

It splits easily, smoothly,
along the perfect lines
of its perfect fibres;
no knots for once.

Nothing else needs to happen
now the birds have begun –
a pair of gulls,
a great northern diver,
a wren.

Back inside, I lay the fire,
put a flame to it.
The heart takes quickly –
bright nest in the grate.

Sometimes a Blackbird Flies from an Oak

After Rilke

Sometimes a blackbird flies from an oak
and keeps on flying, not landing
until it finds the One riding its back.

Then, in the long grass or by the lake,
the unraveling begins to take place.

From the One on the blackbird's back
emerge ten thousand blackbirds,
and from the original flying bird,
one human child.

Fieldfares

The white shadows of the holy – Antonio Machado

The fieldfares are out
on the cold grass,
amongst sodden, baggy leaves.

That yellow-orange spotty breast
and those light chestnut wings
look nice.

But then other birds come
and everything is black and white.

Chacker, chack, chack,
chacker, chack, chack!

Crane

I'm bringing the crane inside
to the kitchen table;
to lay it down, maybe –
yes, to lay it down.

Its white body is grey
or the kitchen light is feeble,
or my eyes are feeble –
yes, my eyes are feeble.

Where I found it, I don't know
but the yard is full of them
and the trees are in bloom
with the white blush of their bodies,
long legs hanging,
hingeing.

I count five more on the doorstep.
They must be from somewhere.

My crane is probably old and male,
though I've no crane knowledge,
except beak (O Mother of God!)
and the peculiar familiarity of eyes.

I lay it down on the old pine,
push the newspapers aside
and wait.

In times of uncertainty,
wait.

The crane's breast sheds its feathers.
They pour off the table
like milk for the cat.

The white of the feather-milk
seeps from his body,
soaks up the papers,
pools on the floor.

In no time, the cranes on the doorstep
merge with the whitewashed door.

I am nowhere to be seen,
something that feels like relief –
yes, it's relief,
like staying home and going out at the same time.

On Waking

I get up,
ease the curtains,
stare outside at the wind.

Anything that's not tied down is gone,
even the sun.

I realise, OK,
there will never be a poem like the side of that hill.

Stillness

Here all is separation, there it was breath —Rainer Maria Rilke

To spend the whole day doing nothing.
To remember how that feels.
To sit outside with the dog and the birds, wet hair steaming in
      the sunlight.
To listen to last night's rain dripping off the trees.
To know this is something I've forgotten
how to do, head always aching with something else.
To sit here in stillness, or thinking about stillness,
or trying to find stillness.
Each blade of grass has a raindrop or two.
Each leaf is falling, has already fallen,
is getting ready to fall.

The Kindness

The kindness of the day
is the white horse that stands in the rain
without words,
eating grass or not eating grass.

The horse is standing below the hill
where the young woods begin
and the river used to flow
two horses deep.

It knows good grass and rain
since these are the days of rain
and the blue-black nights of rain.

The white horse is waiting
for the river to refill,
since these are the days of forever
and the blue-black nights of forever.

The kindness of the night
is the rain that falls on the white horse
without words,
refilling the river or not refilling the river.

Self-Portrait with Snow

A hand-bell is ringing in the woods.
It's making room for the light to bend.
Here and there, where the fall is fresh,
small birds land.

The Foal

The rain was black that morning, red at night,
the day the newborn foal forgot to breathe.
We buried its warm heart by candlelight.

Times like these, we should have burnt the body white,
left nothing of the foal to be retrieved
in rain so black that morning, red at night.

When you bury what you love, there's no respite
and our faces soon began to disbelieve
that we buried its warm heart by candlelight.

Sometimes things are best left out of sight,
like how the heart began to shake and heave
in rain so black that morning, red at night.

It was easy to pick flowers, feign delight
at the softness of the petals and the leaves
as we buried its warm heart by candlelight.

In winter, when the wind was hard and bright
we tiptoed in our coats beside the grave
in rain so black that morning, red at night.

But in the end, the foxes dug the site,
too hungry to remember how to grieve
in rain so black that morning, red at night,
and they swallowed its cold heart by new moonlight.

Because the Moon Is Its Own Bright Country

1

Because the moon is its own bright country,
the man gets up and the woman gets up
to go out and gaze in the warm milk of midsummer
as it hangs and waits, like a lozenge in the night's pale throat,
full enough to soothe the loathing he spoke or the loathing she spoke
into the deep well at the heart of each –
that dark crater that does not know itself,
at least not in the way the moon knows,
because the moon is its own bright country.

2

Because the moon is its own bright country,
it's easy to ignore the single white horse
at Tycho, that brilliant crater in the lunar south,
that wide, dark mouth that speaks only of love
if the woman listens or the man listens, with their heads tilted
to the side like a bird might listen or a dog,
one who knows how to show respect, to look up
to a four-billion-year-old rock – it too in tilted orbit –
because the moon is its own bright country.

3

Because the moon is its own bright country,
the horse is free to sleep and eat and dream,
to canter from one crater to another, to be a horse

without the insistent beetle of the mind, content
to be a horse in the way horses are, without words,
tussling only with the odd rock that trips it
or the occasional visit from the man or the woman,
taking data from a home that is not theirs,
because the moon is its own bright country.

4

Because the moon is its own bright country,
the white horse can never be caught and tethered,
can never be brought to earth to feed on grass –
the moon horse eats rock and coarse mineral rubble,
cavorts with lunar ice and the boiling brightness
of sunlit Mare Crisium, Sea of Crises –
can never be ridden or raced or blinkered
in the way the man and the woman can be,
because the moon is its own bright country.

5

Because the moon is its own bright country,
neither the man nor the woman saves the drowning beetle
from the dog's bowl, neither puts a finger in the dog slobber water
to assist, or submerges a leaf for it to climb out –
the woman does not know and the man does not know
that the dog's bowl is a universe they can serve
easily, quietly, while nobody is looking or praising,
nobody is dedicating poems to them, in the way poets honour the moon
because the moon is its own bright country.

6

Because the moon is its own bright country,
the moon horse will walk with the man and the woman
in their dreams, will guide them from Tycho in the south
to Mare Serenitatis in the north, the Sea of Serenity,
and together they will bathe in the idea of water –
the body is its own bright country – and float for a while,
waiting, hanging in the vast dark expanse
of something other than themselves, something shining,
because the moon is its own bright country.

Horse-Man's Long Dream of the Moon

Horse-Man has stood beneath this tree for three hundred moons.
He's hungry for the milk of the moon, its liquid throat.
Nobody else is here, nobody crosses the line
between Horse-Man and his long dream of the moon.

He lifts up one hoof then puts it back down,
each hoof lifting and replacing,
like a man learning to count.

The moon shines into the dip of Horse-Man's back,
into the flat space between his small, horse ears
and down into his four horse legs.

The air is cold tonight and clear, like time.

Petrichor

Horse-Man is neither greedy nor ascetic,
neither rich nor grovelling.

He knows how to breathe.

When I say to him, 'Where now?'
he kneels down on his front legs
and lowers himself, his back soft
like a woman's back with its curve and its smell.

He is always ready to run fast or to be still.

In his wisdom, heavy rain means walking,
two legs slowly stretching forwards,
then the other two next.

He knows that legs are meant for all things leggy,
in the way the sun is meant to melt ice.

Always motion in the muscle, in the flanks,
in the neck and hair. So much motion
that stillness is eternally there.

I can see it in his happy face
because surely, to walk in heavy rain
is a freedom only some enjoy
and surely, this is a kind of happiness.

If I'm lucky he lets me ride for a long time
and I can watch the night sky make its way inside,
feel the cool night air in his heart.

'Ah,' he sighs, as his hooves move on,
'Aaaah,' he sighs, like an animal. Yes, like that!

If I've eaten too much, Horse-Man will kneel again soon
and drop me, perhaps, at the foot of a tree.
He will nod towards it like a leaf nods
and I'll know he's tired and I am a glutton.

I'll lie down where the earth is still dry
and when I've settled my head
in some dirt and some leaves,
he will walk above me and stand
with his belly rising like an upside-down hill,
over me, over me, over me.

And I will know our enormous safety.

The rain will pour off him for hours.
Horse-Man adores the smell of rain on dry earth.
Horse-Man says: 'She who cannot love rain, cannot yield.'
Never do I ask him to explain.

Horse-Man Will Not Ride

Horse-Man will not ride with me today
since the fields are too wet
or the fields are too dry.

I look at Horse-Man glowing
in his old brown coat,
backlit eyes glistening.
I look at the green fields,
long grass growing.

Still, he is immovable,
in the way blind people with good eyesight
are immovable.

Minutes pass in silence.

If I was clever, I'd say
Horse-Man was showing me field-love.

Horse-Man Says Yes

Horse-Man is always nearer than I think
and wise to my desires – the secret woods, the open hills.

On hot days, he takes me to the very top
and we stand in silence like really quiet flutes,
watch the world pick itself out from the night.
We stand like this for some time,
for no reason.

The hills neither cry nor shake.

Horse-Man on Harris

Horse-Man is lying in the grass, in the bog iris and buttercups. He's easy, glorious, but I can't prove it, except perhaps to the early fisherman with his ropes and old rowboat on the open bay. Perhaps to him or to his boat, I could say that when the sun beats down like this, Horse-Man shines in the buttercups and the bog iris, in the tall lush grass. Perhaps the boat would nod across the bay and perhaps the fisherman would agree and say that when the wind blows – this soft summer breeze – the bog iris move like teeming people in a city move, in random, perfect patterns that mark each one out and then abandon the difference.

Horse-Man in the Dunes

Horse-Man is curled, dog-like,
in a sandy bowl of the dunes,
his body slowly sinking.

I listen as he shuffles his hooves
in the shifting grains, and the wind
blows sand in his thick brown mane.

This is either a birthing or a burial,
body praising this place with flesh,
with horse hair and sweet horse breath.

I curl up alongside him,
my back to his belly like a lover.

Horse-Man at Callanish

Horse-Man settles himself
in the old burial chamber.

The wind scours the stones,
blasts the grass of this bird-less place.

Horse-Man's coat is ruffled.

It's clear, the wind from his nostrils
is the same stony wind, only stronger;
the way his great bulk belongs here,
its pleasing brown solidity,
is the same belonging the stones stand for.

For once, there is no fussing in me.

All the things the wind blows
are blowing in it.

Horse-Man and the Aspens

Three rooks in the lime green poplar –
black lozenges for the morning's throat.

I long to write the words *complexity* and *easy*
love alongside one another,
like the scrawled signature of rooks.

Horse-Man waits while I'm looking,
triangular leaves winking.

The world opens and closes like an eye.
The rooks *aarck* and croak.

Horse-Man and the Oak

This morning Horse-Man is hanging
upside-down (magic rope) in an oak tree,
his hooves moving as though he's running
and the leaves all around him laughing.

Only oak trees could bear this much joy.

To Lie Here in the Dark

To lie here in the dark
where Horse-Man lies,
his body reclined
like a recumbent stone,
the vast hill of his belly
rising and falling
in the invisible world
of this night, somewhere
where suffering is
held in the heart muscle of the animal
like a foetus, curled, already adored
for the new life it will bring.

Horse-Man at Crotha Bothy

Beloved,

First light, fire, tea. I strip-wash at the sink as the moon goes down behind one hill and the sun rises over another. I stand outside on the deck at just after 6 a.m. and the whole glen is silent, utterly sound-less, except for the first calls of small birds and the flowing burn. No wind. The trees are motionless.

I wish never to forget – this is where we come from and return to, at last.

Acknowledgements

Acknowledgements and thanks are due to the editors of *Earthlines* for publishing 'Talking Meat' in 2017. Thanks also to Dark Mountain for publishing 'Horse-Man at Crotha Bothy' in *Dark Mountain 16*, autumn 2019.

I have been entirely remiss about sending any of the other poems anywhere, and so I'm very grateful to Tony Frazer, my editor, for continuing to support my work.

I wish to thank Kath Burlinson, Paul Oertel & Nancy Spanier for their unwavering support and love. I could not have written these poems in 2017 & 2018 if they had not been part of my life.

I would also like to thank all members of the Authentic Artist Collective, who have helped me in innumerable ways to step up and show up again and again. My deep gratitude and love to all AAers, and especially to the PMers.

Hearty thanks to Kate Walters for her cover art image, 'Sentinel', and for continuing to make art that chimes so much with my poetry. Kate's work can be found at http://www.katewalters.co.uk.

Thanks also to Emma Butcher, for her visual art collaboration on 'Crane' for *Mouth*, Atlantic Press, 2018.

Thank you to all members of 12, whose support and inspiration gave birth to many of the poems in this book. I'm deeply appreciative of the wisdom and open sharing of all these women.

I am indebted to Julie Wise for leading me to Omraam Mikhaël Aïvanhov, and to Rach Connor for her deep friendship and for leading me to Patricia Albere.

My most dear husband and our two daughters are the blessed wheat of my daily bread. Thank you.

Lightning Source UK Ltd.
Milton Keynes UK
UKHW011403291219
356034UK00001B/36/P